Original title:
The Frost Between Us

Copyright © 2024 Creative Arts Management OÜ
All rights reserved.

Author: Adeline Fairfax
ISBN HARDBACK: 978-9916-94-518-6
ISBN PAPERBACK: 978-9916-94-519-3

Breaths in the Crystal Air.

We laugh as we shiver, teeth chattering loud,
Our breath forms ice castles, proud and unbowed.
Jokes freeze on our lips, a tall tale to share,
While snowflakes all dance in the crystal air.

Chill of Unspoken Words

Your eyes roll like snowballs, I feign a long sigh,
Each glance is a snowflake, I wonder why.
The chill of our silence wraps tight like a scarf,
Yet laughs burst through the air, so playful and daft.

Icy Veils of Silence

In the frosty morning, we play peek-a-boo,
Behind icy veils of silence, just me and you.
A glance here, a giggle, the cold makes us wise,
We warm up our hearts with the heat of our eyes.

Winter's Breath on Our Hearts

Snowmen unsteady wobble in all the fun,
With winter's breath tickling, we both start to run.
You slip and you tumble, a comical view,
As laughter takes flight, like a bird on the dew.

Frosted Paths We Once Walked

We danced on sidewalks, slips and slides,
Chasing snowflakes, laughter our guides.
With frosty noses, we made our way,
But then you tripped, oh—what a display!

Hot cocoa spilled, our joy turned messy,
We laughed so hard, life felt so zesty.
In snowy lands we'd leave our mark,
But next time, please, no stunts in the park!

Barren Landscapes of Affection

In winter's chill, the heart grew cold,
Emotions wrapped like scarves of old.
We sat on benches, snowflakes flew,
And swore our love was strong and true.

But ice sculptures made of secret fears,
Cracked under laughter, melted tears.
Each joke turned bitter, each smile a test,
Who knew romance could freeze like the rest?

When Hearts Turn to Ice

The heat of summer, we let it go,
Our feelings frosted, just so-so.
Like late-night snacks left in the fridge,
Our chemistry waned, we neared the edge.

You joked, 'We're just a chilly pair,'
I laughed and handed you my spare.
A thermos filled with hot delight,
You took a sip and got the fright!

Shivers of a Forgotten Embrace

Once we cuddled, close and snug,
Now we shiver, it feels like a shrug.
Your icy fingers, I can't explain,
A frosty hug that's driving me insane.

But memories linger, wrapped in chill,
Of laughter shared and a winter thrill.
Let's find the sun, reclaim the warm,
Before we freeze in this frosty storm!

Mornings Wrapped in Winter

Wrapped up tight in puffy gear,
A penguin waddle, let's all cheer!
Hot cocoa spills, oh what a sight,
Watch me skate, then hold on tight!

Snowflakes dance, a frozen song,
But my nose feels oh so wrong.
Slipping, sliding, down I go,
A snowball fight? A real show!

Beyond the Grasp of Thaw

Chasing the sun, it's still too cold,
Out here, we find adventures bold.
Hot soup in hand, but spills like grace,
  Laughter rings in this icy place.

Sleds run wild, like laughter's race,
I'm the king of this snowy space.
But as I trip on my own two feet,
I land in snow—what a cool treat!

Heartbeats Lost in the Cold

Hearts are warm, though noses freeze,
Chocolate smudged on my winter fleece.
Teeth chattering, we laugh aloud,
Together bundled, we feel so proud.

My mittens hide, where did they stray?
Snowball fights make the world okay.
In frosty chaos, we start to build,
A snowman prince with arms all thrilled!

Silently Shattered Bonds

In winter's grip, our chats may freeze,
Yet here I stand, eager to tease.
Under layers, friendships bloom,
Warm laughter navigates the gloom.

We build a fortress made of dreams,
While snowflakes join in giggling streams.
With every slip, with every fall,
Our jokes, like snow, just cover all.

Winter's Embrace of Regret

Snowflakes fall, I slip and slide,
Regrets pile up, like snow, I hide.
Hot cocoa spills, on my new mittens,
I question choices, as winter's smitten.

Frosty air makes my nose so red,
I wish I'd stayed in, wrapped up in bed.
But here I am, in this chilly dance,
Wishing for warmth, a second chance.

Barriers of Ice and Air

You waved hello through icy glass,
I tried to reply, but slipped on grass.
My words got frozen, trapped in the breeze,
While penguins laughed, "Oh, please, oh, please!"

Every snowman judges my feeble plight,
As I tumble down in a laughable fight.
With every slip, I find my grace,
On this slippery stage, I embrace my place.

Across a Sea of Glacial Silence

In the winter hush, we both froze still,
With laughter wrapped in a snowball thrill.
I shouted words, they bounced in place,
Yet looked so silly, I started to chase.

Our giggles filled the frosty air,
Each flake a whisper, a frosty dare.
But silence stole my snowman's smile,
Now I'm stuck here, for a while!

Shadows of a Winter's Day

Shadows dance on this snowy stage,
While I stumble, like an ice age sage.
I trip on shadows, I laugh in vain,
   In winter's grip, it's all a game.

Snowmen mock with their button eyes,
As I make snow angels, full of surprise.
Underneath blankets, I sneakily plot,
To conquer this cold, with a warm pot!

Shivers in the Air

When winter prances, jackets clash,
And noses turn as red as ash.
We giggle while our teeth do chatter,
Who knew that cold could make us scatter?

Snowflakes twirl like dancers bold,
Rumors of warmth just might unfold.
But here we stand, with cocoa cups,
Warming hands, while giving ups!

Glacial Remnants of Love

A heart once warm, now frosty blue,
Sent shivers down to my left shoe.
You said "let's chill," but who would've thought,
That chilly love would leave us caught?

With mittens on, we try to squeeze,
A hug that's lost in winter's freeze.
Our laughter echoes, a sound so sweet,
Two pals slipping on snow, not on their feet!

A Chasm of Cold

Between us lies a frozen stream,
Where sparkles shine and icebergs dream.
We throw snowballs, but miss the mark,
Our timing's off; maybe it's dark?

It's hard to bridge this chilly gap,
When your breath's vapor's a frosty trap.
But we'll build a snowman, tall and stout,
And melt this gap with joy, no doubt!

Snowfall on Forgotten Paths

The pathway's white like memories lost,
We trip on hopes, but what a cost!
Each flake's a laugh, a fleeting call,
While slipping and sliding, we risk our fall.

What was once clear is now a blur,
With every tumble, let's not deter.
For friendship's warmth will always find,
The snow-y ways that intertwined!

The Chill of What Was

Once we laughed till we cried,
Now we just stare and hide.
You built walls of ice and stone,
I warm up with a frozen cone.

Your jokes are just snowflakes now,
Melting slowly, I don't know how.
We used to dance, now we freeze,
Is it winter? Or a cold breeze?

Bring me back those sunny days,
Where goofy smiles lit up our plays.
Instead, I'm left with frosty sighs,
And chilling stares that don't surprise.

Here's a toast to our old cheer,
With hot cocoa in a frosty sphere.
Let's laugh at our frigid fate,
When did dating feel like fate?

Glacial Hearts Adrift

You threw me a snowball once,
Now I'm dodging frozen dunce.
You plan ice castles in the air,
But I'm stuck in winter's glare.

Glaciers move faster than this date,
Your smile's sealed in a frosty crate.
I'd rather chase a running hare,
Than sit here in this frozen stare.

Your wit is like an icicle,
Sharp and cold, but that's the thrill.
Let's thaw out this heart of stone,
And find warmth where love has grown.

So come on, let's slip and slide,
And see what melts on this joyride.
We'll break the ice with our own twists,
Forget the chill, let's make a list!

Snow-Draped Desires

Under layers of sparkling white,
We lost the spark that felt so right.
Your puns are colder than the ground,
But I'm still searching for joy around.

You say I'm frigid, hard to read,
But your punchlines plant a growing seed.
Let's unwrap this pack of snow,
And see how much our laughter can grow.

We could ski or just fall flat,
Your idea of fun is where it's at.
Wrapped in layers, feeling small,
Let's ignite the heat and start a brawl!

With sleds and snowmen, we'll create,
A winter wonder that's first-rate.
Let's chuck the chill, embrace the fire,
And melt our hearts with silly desire.

Enigmas Wrapped in Ice

You're a riddle wrapped in ice,
A puzzle that no joke can slice.
Your thoughts are like frosty nights,
Dancing shadows with blinking lights.

Each smile a snowflake in disguise,
Comes crashing down, what a surprise!
We fumble with words, take a try,
Like frozen fish—where's the pie?

I say let's thaw those clever lines,
With puns and laughs, let's break confines.
Though we chill like winter's breath,
Let's embrace humor till we're deaf!

So here's to us, two frosty goofs,
Trying hard to find our hoots and hoofs.
Let's laugh till our ice melts away,
And find warmth in this silly ballet.

Fields of Frozen Desire

In fields where laughter's found,
Snowflakes dance, all around.
Penguins on a frosty spree,
Laughing at us, can't you see?

Icicles that bend and sway,
Wishing winter's chill away.
But hot cocoa's worth a fight,
Even snowmen know delight!

A snowball here, a slip on ice,
Oh, winter, you're so chill, so nice.
With mittens thick and scarves all bright,
We giggle through the frosty night.

But when the snow makes us a mess,
Warmed hearts can't avoid the stress.
Yet still we slide and tumble true,
In fields where winter brings me you.

Where Hearts Remain Frostbitten

In a world of icy stares,
Where love is caught unawares.
Mittens trap our hands in wool,
While snowflakes make a grand old fool.

With frozen toes, we stumble 'round,
Puddles turn to icy ground.
Yet here we stand with smiles so wide,
Trying hard our warmth to hide.

Our date's a skate across the pond,
But none of us are very fond.
We trip and laugh, our cheeks so red,
A frosty love to keep instead.

But as the winter breezes blow,
Our hearts defrost, this we know.
In frozen laughter, love ignites,
Two hearts warmed on coldest nights.

When Warmth Meets the Cold

The moment warmth collides with chill,
We giggle at the winter thrill.
Sipping tea while snowflakes fall,
With everyday fun, we stand tall.

In a world draped in white delight,
We dance through every frosty night.
But hold my hand or I might freeze,
A shiver like a sneeze, oh please!

But cuddling close 'neath blankets thick,
With hot soup, we share the trick.
Winter games become our show,
As laughter warms the frost and snow.

So with each grin and playful shove,
We find the spark, the winter love.
Here's to laughter in the cold,
A funny tale of hearts so bold!

The Distance in Winter's Grip

In winter's clutch, a chilly pie,
We wave from far, oh me, oh my!
But snowmen stand, they take our place,
As we throw snowballs with a grace.

With shivers shared from way on high,
Our laughter echoes, reaches sky.
Yet somehow each clear winter's night,
Brings warmth that makes our spirits bright.

Slipping here and sliding there,
We tumble in this frosty air.
With rosy cheeks, we jest and tease,
Finding joy as winter's breeze.

So let the cold wind blow away,
We'll laugh together, come what may.
Through frosty fun, our hearts align,
Even far apart, you still are mine.

Cold Hands, Warm Memories

When winter comes, my fingers freeze,
Yet your laugh warms me like summer's breeze.
Thoughts of cocoa and snowy grace,
Remind me of our happy place.

We built a snowman, round and stout,
He lost a nose, guess what that's about?
Your mittens mismatched, a funny sight,
Yet in cold chaos, everything feels right.

Sipping tea as frost bites the pane,
We giggle at snowflakes that dance like rain.
Each chilly breath, a misty plume,
Yet inside, the heart knows no gloom.

As we recount our snowy mishaps,
Laughter erupts, like warm weather naps.
Those frozen days became our lore,
Cold hands, warm hearts, forever more.

Crystalized Moments of Separation

In the chill, our breath forms a cloud,
Yet it's your jokes that make me so proud.
We stumble through drifts, slipping like fools,
With every fall, we break all the rules.

A snowball fight goes terribly wrong,
You ducked too late—what a classic gong!
We laugh so hard, the neighbors peek,
These frozen moments, the ones we seek.

Watching footprints fade in the white,
Like our plans that slipped out of sight.
Yet every laugh that we still share,
Turns that distance into thin air.

So as the ice on our hearts may form,
Your goofy grin keeps my soul warm.
Though separated by miles of snow,
In every chill, our memories glow.

Hushed echoes in the Snow

In the stillness, our giggles bounce,
As soft as snowflakes, they twirl and flounce.
We raced through white, with joy and cheer,
Yet tripped on twigs—oh my, dear, dear!

Your mitten caught in a branchy snare,
We wrestled with laughter, without a care.
Amidst the quiet, our joy takes flight,
Echoes of warmth on a frosty night.

We watched the stars with noses red,
Roasting marshmallows while sharing bread.
Whispers of warmth in the cooling air,
Even in winter, there's love everywhere.

So let the shivers come in flurries,
With soft chuckles swirling in a hurry.
For every chill that nips my nose,
Is wrapped in warmth wherever love goes.

The Silence of a Winter Moon

Under the moon, the world turns white,
The silence giggles, oh what a sight!
We stomp on crusts with boots too big,
With every crunch, we feel the jig.

You swear you saw a yeti prance,
But it's just the neighbor's dog in trance.
We share secrets where the snowflakes dwell,
In our goofy bubble, all is swell.

Yet even in quiet, we've known some strife,
As freezing toes remind us of life.
But our laughter echoes through the gloom,
In the glow of winter, there's always room.

So here's to the moments, both silly and bright,
When the world feels heavy, we take to flight.
In the darkness, your smile is my tune,
We dance in the shadows of a winter moon.

Lingering in Subzero Spaces

In the cold where we stand,
Our breath makes clouds expand.
You laugh and then I sneeze,
We both freeze like the trees.

Your nose is red and bright,
Yet you claim it feels just right.
We dance like penguins on ice,
But we both know it's not so nice.

You say hot cocoa will save,
While we pretend to be brave.
I slip and make a wild sound,
And we both fall on the ground.

Oh, these temps, they're so high,
Yet we're laughing as we fly.
In this winter's endless jest,
You're my frostbitten treasure chest.

Frosted Hopes of Tomorrow

We dream of sunny skies,
While wearing woolen ties.
The sun just won't appear,
So let's drink more of this beer.

You say snowflakes are unique,
But I can hardly speak.
My lips are chapped and dry,
As I choke back a sigh.

We build a snowman so tall,
It takes a nifty brawl.
With its carrot nose all wrong,
We laugh and sing a song.

Tomorrow we'll break the freeze,
And trade our jackets with ease.
Until then, let's share this cheer,
While we turn our giggles to gear.

Solitude in Icy Silence

In the quiet of the night,
Snowflakes dance, oh what a sight!
Alone, I sip my tea,
And wonder where you'd be.

A chill runs down my spine,
Oh wait, that's just the wine!
I sit here, cheeks aglow,
And search for heat below.

Your texts start to appear,
Each one brings a cheer.
You hate the cold like me,
But laugh at destiny.

As icicles start to fall,
I can hear your voice call.
In solitude, we're tight,
For winter brings delight.

Chill of Memories Past

Remember when we built that fort?
Our snowballs flew like sport.
You claimed to have no aim,
But won the snowy game.

Time has flown, now we freeze,
In this chill, it's all a tease.
You trip and then you shout,
Each slip brings silly doubt.

Your laughter fills the air,
As you fall into my chair.
With snowflakes on your nose,
We cherish how it goes.

Memories wrapped in snow,
Are warm in hearts, you know?
So let's embrace this cold,
And let our stories unfold.

Dreams Crystalled in Snow

Snowflakes are whispers, oh so shy,
They dance and they twirl, then say goodbye.
Hats fly off heads, a comedic sight,
While everyone slips, oh what a fright!

Mittens mismatched, like friends who fight,
We laugh and we stumble, it feels so right.
Snowmen with noses made of old shoes,
Tell tales of winter's silly snooze.

Through a Glass of Ice

Peering through frost, my breath does show,
It's foggy outside, but the inside's aglow.
Windows like mirrors for winter's style,
But my face makes them smudge—oh, what a trial!

I wave to the snowman, he waves back, too,
His carrot nose droops, just like my shoe.
A comedy sketch on this icy stage,
Where every misstep earns a winter wage.

The Coldness of Parting

Bundled up tight, but it's hard to part,
Our hugs turn to penguin waddle art.
With slippery steps and laughter loud,
We bark at the cold like a stubborn crowd.

Sleds fly nearby, a face full of snow,
One tumble, one roll, how low can we go?
As ice breaks beneath us, we slide, then fall,
Like two clumsy seals, let's laugh through it all!

Distant Horizons of Frost

The horizon is frosty, seen through the haze,
Where laughter and snowball fights seek to amaze.
Toboggans zoom past, like a racecar's roar,
As we gather the ice for a snow-plough war.

In mittens too small, we fumble and glide,
Frosty faces beam as the cold takes its ride.
With cocoa in hand, and a cheer in our soul,
We'll conquer the winter, that's our ultimate goal!

Permafrost of the Heart

Your heart's so cold, it might just freeze,
I thought we had warmth, but now I sneeze.
We're wrapped in ice, a chilly embrace,
Wishing for sun, yet stuck in this place.

Your smile's a snowflake, it melts away,
But not before it gives me dismay.
You laughed so hard, it slipped on a patch,
Now here we are, no love to dispatch.

We dance on ice, but feet start to slip,
With every giggle, I lose my grip.
The wind keeps howling, our cheeks turned blue,
Yet here we stand, just me and you.

Though winter bites and jackets we wear,
We stumble through snow without a care.
In the freeze of love, we might just thaw,
Your frosty heart's the secret I draw.

Glaze Over Memories

Remember the time we built a grand fort?
It melted away, just like my retort.
We slapped on snowballs, a comical fight,
Then slipped on the ice, both out of sight.

Your quirky jokes have too much chill,
They drop like icicles, give me a thrill.
We sip hot cocoa, but the mugs are cold,
As we chuckle and laugh, getting bold.

I try to recall how we used to sizzle,
But all I get now is a frosty drizzle.
In this glaze of past, our laughter persists,
Concocting ice puns, it's hard to resist.

So let's embrace this wintry fate,
And make snow angels, we won't be late.
As memories freeze, we'll thaw out our glee,
With silly antics, just you and me.

Snowbound Dreams

In dreams of snowflakes, we slip and slide,
Chasing each other like kids on a ride.
Snowbound and cozy, under warm blankets,
You stealing the covers, oh, how my heart sankes!

We set out on sleds, racing downhill,
But my laughter ends with a comical spill.
The snowflakes fall like soft little laughs,
Tickling our noses, offering gaffs.

A snowman stands with a lopsided grin,
With carrots for noses, and mischief within.
How did we get lost in this wintery haze?
Cold and contradictory, run all our days.

Yet here we are, in this chilly delight,
Making warm memories while spirits take flight.
Through snowbound dreams that softly entwine,
We'll laugh through the winter, your heart next to mine.

Bittersweet Winter's Grasp

Your hand's an icicle; mine's turning blue,
Yet we're caught in the winter, stuck like glue.
With coats so puffy, we waddle around,
As laughter erupts, our warmth has been found.

The chill in the air makes me turn bright red,
With each little joke, it's like warmth instead.
Our snowball fights are a mix of jest,
With cold little hands, we'll play our best.

Yet here's the deal, I can't feel my toes,
In this icy dance, how the laughter grows.
Wrapped in layers, we snicker and tease,
Even the winter's chill can't bring us unease.

So bring on the snowflakes; let them unfurl,
In this bittersweet grasp, let our hearts twirl.
We'll frolic and giggle through frostbites and glee,
In the coldest of seasons, you and me.

Layered in Ice and Time

Layers of laughter, frozen tight,
We slip and slide, what a sight!
Hiccups of joy, snowflakes flare,
Our chilly jokes hang in the air.

Mittens mismatched, a fashion bluff,
Warmed chocolate drinks, just enough!
We giggle, like kids in the snow,
Building our castles, row by row.

Costumes of winter, hats askew,
A frosty frolic, just us two!
Chasing each other, slipping and spin,
In this freeze frame, where do we begin?

Our hearts are warm, though tempers freeze,
Tickled by winter's playful tease.
While ice might chill the world outside,
In this frosty fun, we take pride!

The Coolness of Unsaid Words

With pockets full of snow and fun,
We juggle the silence, a game begun.
Your eyes, they twinkle, a frosty jest,
Words hang in the air, a playful quest.

Snowmen nodding, know our tune,
Giggles dance 'round like a cartoon.
Frozen quips like ice in the sun,
While whispers melt, our hearts still run.

We skim over feelings, with frosty flair,
In this glacial silence, we twirl in the air.
Stumbling through laughter, we're caught in a freeze,
Dodging our feelings with graceful ease.

Chilly exchanges, a breezy game,
Chattering hearts, but no one to blame.
With each sip of warmth, we find our way,
In this frosty frolic, we laugh and play!

Chilled Connections

I tossed a snowball; you ducked just in time,
Your flare for dodging should be a crime!
Frozen remarks and silly retorts,
Laughing so hard, we forgot our courts.

Epic snow forts, the war has begun,
Pelting our past with laughter and fun.
Each chilly glance, a chuckle arrives,
In this frosty playground, our humor thrives.

Tangled in scarves, we trip in the snow,
Your frosty stares, they steal the show!
Hot cocoa sipped, and marshmallows tossed,
In our icy melee, we never feel lost.

Underneath blankets, we giggle away,
With whispers of shivers and words gone astray.
A friendship woven through winter's delight,
In this chilled connection, we shine ever bright!

Fragments of a Hallowed Past

Once upon ice, we danced with glee,
Fragments of chuckles, just you and me.
The echoes of snowballs still float in the breeze,
As we wander on paths piled high with freeze.

The scarf that you lost is tangled in time,
But we warm it with laughter, oh so sublime!
In the city of frost, we learned the cold,
Wrapped up in memories, worth more than gold.

Your mittens are silly, bright green and blue,
Each ball of snow is a story anew.
From the slips and the trips to the giggles that soar,
In this hallowed past, we always want more.

Though frost may layer the laughs that we share,
This bond forged in winter is beyond compare.
So raise up your cup of hot joy, keep it close,
In the warmth of our past, we thrive the most!

A Truce of Frozen Memories

In a fridge, we stashed our dreams,
With ice cubes clinking, or so it seems.
We shared a laugh about old times,
While penguins danced in silly rhymes.

The snowmen smiled with carrot grins,
As we debated who truly wins.
Hot cocoa spilled, a playful fight,
Chasing each other through the night.

With jackets on, we braved the chill,
Inventing games, our laughter still.
Each frosty breath a cloud of cheer,
Memories brewed with every beer.

A truce was born in winter's clasp,
With silly faces, we'd often gasp.
Frozen moments, we can't outgrow,
No winter storm could fade our glow.

Beneath the Slumbering Snow

Beneath the layers, dreams do snore,
Like sleepy bears who crave some more.
Snowflakes twirl like they're in a show,
While we chuckle, letting memories flow.

Under blankets, we plot and scheme,
Building forts from the frozen theme.
Sneaky snowballs fly with glee,
As winter whispers, 'Come play with me!'

With frosty frolics, we leap and bound,
While squirrels scold us from the ground.
Snow angels made, a sight so bright,
In this chilly land, it feels just right.

We snicker softly at winter's grace,
Two frozen friends, a favorite place.
Joyfully wrapped in chilly bliss,
Nostalgia dances with each soft kiss.

Moments That Never Thawed

In the cold room filled with laughter,
Each frosty moment, a joyful chapter.
With every giggle and sassy retort,
We write stories of winter sport.

Wearing mittens like elegant art,
Throwing snowballs with all our heart.
In frozen battles we claim our ground,
While frosty chuckles truly abound.

Here, moments freeze, yet they won't fade,
Every joke and prank well laid.
In the chilly air, warmth to find,
As joy and laughter intertwine.

We gather round with mugs of cheer,
Sipping warmth to chase the fear.
In this room where our hearts may bloom,
The memories linger, dispelling gloom.

Silent Cries in a Cold Room

In the quiet house, an echo's hiss,
A snowstorm's tantrum we can't dismiss.
Muffled laughter behind closed doors,
While snowflakes create their frozen floors.

Each sigh we breathe, a chilly sound,
Mournful whispers of joy profound.
Under ice, our secrets lie,
With frozen grins, we won't comply.

Hot chocolate's a remedy for the freeze,
As warmth-filled jokes aim to please.
The cold may bite, but so does fate,
In this room we absolutely celebrate.

With every chuckle, we thaw our woes,
Making the best of winter's shows.
So here we are, let the fun resume,
In our hearts, we banish the gloom.

Icy Stares and Silent Sighs

In a café, we sit apart,
With glances sharp, like frozen art.
Your coffee's hot, my ice is cold,
But words you're storing, not yet told.

Outside, the snowflakes dance and twirl,
Diehard lovers in a frosty swirl.
I shuffle my feet, you tap your mug,
What's brewing here? A heart or a shrug?

Both pretending, it's quite the sport,
With secret plans and little rapport.
A misplaced smile, a cheeky grin,
Are we warming up or freezing in?

So raise a toast to this frozen scene,
Where humor cracks, beneath the sheen.
If only warmth could bridge this gap,
We'd trade our ice for a cozy nap!

Frostbite of the Soul

Beneath the surface, we're a chilled pair,
With frozen jokes that linger in air.
Your roast chicken's good, my soup's too grim,
We laugh it off, on a frosty whim.

You say I'm icy, I say you're blue,
Throwing snowballs of sarcastic view.
My heart's encased in a winter coat,
But you sure make me laugh, even remote.

We bantered on, like each other's thaw,
Neighbors raise brows, their eyes in awe.
Two frosty figures, in love's lost heat,
With every chuckle, we admit defeat.

So here's to heart lessons, utterly absurd,
Like winter spoons dancing without a word.
In this chilly game, our laughter glows,
Who knew frozen hearts could heat up prose?

Crystals in the Void

In the dead of winter, we take a stand,
Two statues made of frosty bland.
You're an ice cube wrapped in a joke,
As snowflakes gather, the day's bespoke.

You throw a wink, I scoff in glee,
A clumsy dance, just you and me.
Your words crackle, like ice on the lake,
My heart giggles, but for goodness' sake!

Crystals form in every silence,
We measure warmth, with no compliance.
Around us spins a chilly charm,
Who knew frozen hearts could disarm?

Thunderous laughs break through the chill,
In splintered smiles, we find our thrill.
So here's to us, in our winter space,
A frosty jest, in a tender embrace!

Surrendering to the Cold

I'm bundled tight in old woolen threads,
While you sparkle like ice, full of dreads.
We talk like snowmen with carrot noses,
In this tundra of thoughts, nobody dozes.

You cracked a smile, it slipped like hail,
I caught your joy, like a wobbly sail.
With jokes that chill and laughter that bites,
We waddle around in our snowball fights.

Surrendering here, we thaw and freeze,
Negotiating warmth, as we tease.
Our hearts are shields, a whimsical sight,
A dance on the edge of a frostbite night.

So let's embrace this frosty affair,
With quirky smiles we willingly share.
The cold may linger, but so does the fun,
In the kingdom of frost, we both are one!

Frozen Echoes of Love

Once we danced in summer's light,
Now we slip on ice at night.
You threw snowballs, I just ducked,
Blew a kiss, and then I plucked.

We built a love of frosty cheer,
But now we freeze, my dear, oh dear!
Your warm laugh is an icy stare,
Like snowflakes caught in a chill-filled air.

Hot cocoa dreams, but winter's here,
Where warmth is just a memory, clear.
I say, "Let's cuddle, you say, "No!"
How'd we end up with this frosty show?

A pop quiz of frozen hearts,
How to thaw these cold, cold parts?
With every giggle, a bit of chill,
You laugh, I sigh, this is a thrill!

Whispers in a Frigid Void

In a land where warmth is rare,
I whisper jokes into the air.
You chuckle lightly, lips so tight,
A frozen grin in the pale moonlight.

Ice pellet puns bounce off your nose,
Like little snowflakes, who knows where it goes?
Your smile's stuck like snow on a tree,
As we dance to the tune of icy glee.

I tried to melt your frosty gaze,
But you just hit me with a frost-laced phrase.
"Why don't we skate on love's thin ice?"
"Because I've tripped, and I've paid that price!"

Our hearts are whispers in the cold,
Funny tales in the night, retold.
Warming words that freeze and thaw,
Together lost in this chill-filled awe.

Shards of Fractured Connection

We're like shards of glass beneath the snow,
A stumble here, a slip, oh no!
Your frosty winks cause my heart to race,
But you won't warm up, what a race!

I tried to send you heat with puns,
Yet every joke ends with frozen runs.
"Do we play this game of chilly fate?"
"Sure, just don't let the icecube wait!"

Each argument drips like melting ice,
And every laugh is like a roll of dice.
You're frosty fun, I'm quirky flair,
In this run of laughs, we spark and glare.

Yet somehow, this cage of ice,
Has made our frosty chaos nice.
We're two odd snowmen in the park,
Chucking snowballs, igniting a spark!

Snowflakes on Distant Souls

Your glance, a snowflake, oh so sweet,
But the chill sends me shivers down to my feet.
We toss around quotes, like snow in the air,
Each one falling with a frosty flare.

One moment we're laughing, the next, a freeze,
In this frosty world, it's hard to tease.
Your smile melts like frost on grass,
But winter comes; will this moment pass?

I dream of spring while we skip on ice,
Wishing one day for warmth that's nice.
Yet here we are, with shivers and jokes,
Creating fun from winter's pokes.

Snowflakes land on our distant souls,
Taking jabs at this funny stroll.
Together we freeze, laugh, and play,
Blizzards may come, but we'll find a way!

Thawing the Longing Heart

My heart's a snowman melting slow,
It laughs when the sun starts to show.
With warm hugs from friends, it starts to thaw,
Yet still wears a scarf, just because!

Ice cubes dance in my coffee cup,
Wiggling about, they're never stuck.
They join me for laughs, a joyous crew,
Who knew frozen hearts could be so blue?

The thermostat's set to 'get it right',
But my heart seems stuck in a chilly night.
I joke with the warmth that opens the door,
"Who needs a summer, when there's so much more?"

Even socks on my feet feel like ice,
But a tickle fights back; oh, it's quite nice!
Let's thaw this heart, let's break the mold,
With laughter and love, bright and bold!

In the Wake of a Cold Dawn

When morning breaks in a frosty hue,
I slip on my socks—they're mismatched too!
The sun peeks in, a cheeky tease,
Saying, 'Get up!' with a playful breeze.

Coffee spills in the winter's grip,
I watch it dance, take a little trip.
"Melt away," I tell my cup,
"Let's start the day, come warm me up!"

My bed's a glacier, too tough to leave,
But who needs warmth when I can believe?
I'll stay in pajamas and laugh out loud,
In this frosty kingdom, I'm pawing a cloud!

Icicles dangle like ornaments fair,
They're laughing at me from up in the air.
"Join us!" they whisper with chilly glee,
I'll dance with you, if you dance with me!

Ice-Covered Affections

My heart's on ice, a figure skater's dream,
Top hat and tails, oh what a team!
With winks and giggles, we glide through the day,
Trying not to slide, oh what ballet!

Cupid's arrows stuck in the freeze,
His bow's gone numb; oh what a tease!
He tried to thaw things with jokes and charm,
But slipped on the ice—didn't mean any harm!

Snowflakes drift down like little slow jesters,
Tickling my nose, silly little testers.
In this ballet of frosty embrace,
Laughter's the warmth that saves face!

Hot cocoa's calling, I know what to do,
We'll sip it together, me and my crew.
Let's gather and giggle beneath the bright stars,
Ice-coated love—no need for cold bars!

Hidden Beneath the Snow

Beneath the drifts, where secrets reside,
A snowman named Fred likes to hide.
He tells me jokes as the winter winds blow,
His carrot nose winks, all covered in snow!

Laughter's buried like a treasure chest,
I dig it out—it's a frosty fest!
With each icy scoop, a grin breaks forth,
Who knew cold hearts could have such worth?

The squirrels are plotting a snowball fight,
While I'm stuck here, wrapped up tight.
But once I break free from my blanket cocoon,
I'll join the mayhem, oh, it'll be a boon!

So we'll frolic and tumble, a crowd of cheer,
With snowflakes like sprinkles, we'll dance without fear.
Even cold can't stop this bubbling flair,
Joy's hidden away, just waiting to share!

Chill of Distant Hearts

Your smile's like winter, cool and bright,
I wave from afar, in frostbitten flight.
We trade cold glances, like snowflakes' dance,
Yet, oh my dear, it's just a chance!

Hot cocoa's brewing, but we're far apart,
I peek through the window, it's a cold heart art.
You laugh at the snowmen, made of old hats,
But I can't quite grasp these chilly spats!

Let's heat up this winter, with some good cheer,
Bring marshmallows and jokes to dispel the drear.
In your frosty presence, I jest and tease,
With snowball fights, let's bury the freeze!

So grab your mittens, let's break through this chill,
We'll melt distant hearts, if you've got the will.
Under the snowflakes, we'll laugh and play,
And toast to this winter, come what may!

Frosted Echoes

In the land of ice, we can't warm a thing,
Your voice, it echoes, like a distant ring.
I throw a snowball, you duck and you frown,
Yet you can't escape this wintertown!

The air's full of giggles, yet frozen with doubt,
I'm trying to thaw this chill all about.
You're wrapped up in wool, a snowflake queen,
But I'll crack a smile, before we've seen!

Ice cubes in glasses, we toast to our fate,
Finding warm moments while we wait and wait.
Let's build up a fire from these frosty woes,
And laugh off the winter, that nobody knows!

So let's stitch together a quilt of delight,
With threads of our laughter, let's banish the night.
In the chilly air, memories will sprout,
As we warm distant whispers, and toss them about!

Winter's Silent Divide

Two hearts like glaciers, carved from the cold,
Moving so slowly, tales left untold.
We wave from the distance, like old movie stars,
But this frosty silence just builds up the bars.

Should we break out the cocoa, or stick to the freeze?
I ponder your smile, hoping it'll tease.
Your snowflake-filled aura can make my heart melt,
Yet here I just stand, with no warmth to be felt.

With mittens and laughter, let's skate down the lane,
I'll trade you a wink, if you promise no pain.
In this winter's game, let's twist and let twirl,
For frozen hearts can, indeed, give a whirl!

So come take my hand, let's break this old mold,
We'll conquer the silence, in stories retold.
With humor and warmth, we'll weather the cold,
And dance through the winter, our own legends bold!

Icy Veins of Silence

Caught in this freeze, like popsicles stuck,
Your smile's like sunshine, yet I feel the yuck.
We stand on the sidewalk, a comical sight,
Can we laugh this cold off, before it's night?

With icicles hanging, we joke through the chill,
Trading shivers and warmth with glances that thrill.
Each breath forms a cloud, a frosty charade,
Yet laughter can thaw these ice-cold cascades!

So let's shape a snowman, with hats out of style,
And roll in the snow, just for a while.
In the heart of winter, there's fun yet to find,
As we chip at the ice, leave the silence behind!

Let's bubble some laughter, our own little spree,
As we dance through the snow like it's made for we.
With humor and cheer, we'll bridge this great gap,
And warm up our hearts in a frosty mishap!

The Long Winter of Our Love

Two hearts are wrapped in blankets tight,
But cuddles can't replace the bite.
Each chilly breeze our whispers find,
Like snowflakes, softly falling, blind.

We bicker over heated drinks,
While ice forms on the kitchen sinks.
Our love's a snowman built too high,
With arms of twigs that wave goodbye.

Hot cocoa's sweet, yet bitter too,
Like jokes we share that leave a bruise.
We laugh until the tea does spill,
Yet here we are, it's winter still.

So let's pretend this chill ain't real,
And dance around as we conceal.
The thermostat sets our hearts aglow,
While coldness reigns outside the window.

Barriers Built by Time

You take your time, you take your space,
While I just slide from place to place.
Our calendars are stacked like ice,
With dates so far, they can't suffice.

You call it patience, I call it slow,
A glacier's pace, a frosty show.
We text in code, with frosty wit,
Like penguins trying to do a split.

Tick-tock, tick-tock, the clock delays,
In frozen fields of yesterdays.
So here we sit, with tea and laughs,
While time moves on, and winter halves.

Love's mixed messages, a snowy maze,
Like trying to see through winter's haze.
We bumble forth, a comical pair,
Defrosting moments, a breath of air.

Reflections in a Frozen Pond

I glance at you through icy glass,
Your funny face, a frozen mass.
Reflections tell of love's sweet tease,
Like winter's chill, it doesn't freeze.

We glide and slip like pups on ice,
With laughter loud, it feels so nice.
Your skates may squeak, your skills may lapse,
Yet every tumble brings loud claps.

The pond we dance has stories told,
Of frozen dreams and hearts so bold.
Our fancy moves may lack some flair,
But twirls and strife make quite a pair.

So let's embrace this frosty heart,
And skip around till spring's sweet start.
In laughter's glow, beneath the sun,
We'll melt away, two souls as one.

Beneath the Frosty Exterior

You think I'm cold, you think I'm tough,
But inside there's warmth, it's just too rough.
Like icebergs floating, pure and wide,
A quip, a laugh—my heart's inside.

Your jokes hit hard, like snowball fights,
Yet when we clash, it always bites.
Beneath the surface, teasing glare,
Are blushing cheeks and yonder flare.

Behind the frost, where passions freeze,
Are playful hearts that skip with ease.
With every glance, we share the chill,
Yet warmth surrounds us, always will.

So let's embrace this funny guise,
And laugh until we melt the skies.
For underneath this icy jest,
Is love's bright flame, and we are blessed.

Cold Touches of Regret

In winter's grasp, we shiver and shake,
Remembering warmth, what a silly mistake.
You wrapped me in layers, a snuggly delight,
Now I trudge through snow like a snowman in fright.

With each little snowflake that lands on my nose,
I recall our love, how it bloomed like a rose.
But now it's all frozen, like ice in my drink,
I laugh at the mess, oh, how did we blink?

You said, "Bundle up!" with a smile like a thief,
While I laughed so hard, all I met was the grief.
Now I wear mittens as big as my heart,
Who knew love's chill would tear us apart?

So here's to the moments, the fun and the freeze,
I'll sigh through the winter, while sipping hot peas.
With bitter regret, I'll toast with some cheer,
To love in the snow—may it disappear!

Winter's Veil Over Us

Beneath winter's wonder, we slip and we slide,
You promise me warmth, but you just want to hide.
Wrapped up like a burrito, I shuffle around,
While you laugh through the window, my misery found.

A snowball in hand, with a grin on your face,
You launch it with glee, I can't finish this race.
Why's it so funny? Oh, the laughter's so real,
As I tumble through snow, what a slippery deal!

We both took for granted our cozy abode,
But now here we dance on this icy road.
You twirl like a ballerina, oh what a sight,
While I pull a muscle, avoiding the fight.

So cheer me on, darling, through this frozen land,
Perhaps we can find a warm place, hand in hand.
But if we keep slipping, I might just take flight,
As snowflakes keep falling, into endless night!

Shattered by the Chill

In a frozen tundra, our dreams went to sleep,
You claimed I was cold, but your blankets were cheap.
With nights full of shivers, I pondered our fate,
You looked so warm, while I felt second rate.

Our laughter echoed, like icicles clink,
You tossed me a snowball, I may need to rethink.
With each little giggle, another toe froze,
And yet, here we are, caught in love's throes.

Your jokes are like snowflakes, some land with a cheer,
While others just drape like white coats of fear.
I tried for a moment to muster a grin,
But all that I felt was the chill creeping in.

So let's raise a toast to the frost on our hearts,
To the giggles and shivers, where humor imparts.
With mittens and scarves, we'll plow through this mess,
May our love be warmer, despite the cold stress!

Echoes of a Frozen Embrace

Your hug is a glacier, a chill I can't take,
I smile through my teeth, as my bones start to ache.
Remember that time when you said, "Cuddle tight!"
But all I felt was the sting of the night.

We twirled in the snow, like pros in a show,
Your dance was so lovely, but I couldn't follow.
My toes turned to ice, my hopes down the drain,
Yet laughter arose from this frosty domain.

With every cold kiss, my lips had to pout,
Who knew that a winter could bring such a drought?
Yet here in this moment, we belt out our tunes,
As snowflakes make music beneath winter moons.

So here's to the laughter, the giggles we share,
May we brave the cold with a warm-hearted flair.
In this freezing ballet, our spirits ignite,
With echoes of joy, we will dance through the night!

Glimmers of Heat in the Ice

Chilly winds can make us funny,
But your warm smile is like money.
A cup of cocoa, a silly dance,
Let's melt this chill with a wild prance.

Snowflakes twirl like giggling sprites,
As we chase each other, silly fights.
Hot cocoa spills, laughter flies,
Who knew ice could bring such highs?

Slippery paths and awkward falls,
Our laughter echoes through winter's halls.
With every slip, we find delight,
Turning frost into purest light.

So here we are, two frozen souls,
In the chill, we find our roles.
Let's spark a fire, make it bright,
With giggles that warm the longest night.

Unraveled Threads of Solitude

Lonely nights wrap me in white,
A quilt of silence, oh what a sight!
But then you show up, making me laugh,
We unravel chill like a cozy scarf.

Your silly jokes melt the gloom,
Like sunbeams chasing winter's doom.
In solitude, we set our sights,
On silly things that bring delights.

The snowman's got a lopsided grin,
He laughs with us, joins in the din.
With each hot soup and each warm toast,
We toast to laughter, oh we boast!

In the frost, we dance so free,
No lonely threads, just you and me.
Let's knit our joy like a vibrant thread,
Unraveled warmth 'til we're well-fed.

Echoes of a Frigid Night

The moonlight sparkles, icy bright,
But your jokes turn cold to warm delight.
We whisper secrets in snow's embrace,
Leaving frosty traces on each face.

Snowflakes fall like whispered lies,
As we stifle giggles beneath the skies.
Each chilly wind brings a new jest,
In this icy realm, we feel so blessed.

A snowball flies, a playful aim,
Turns winter's chill into a game.
With every laugh, we stoke the fire,
Heat from mishaps, our hearts aspire.

So let the winter come and stay,
With you by my side, we'll laugh and play.
In echoes of chill, we'll find our cheer,
With fun and frolic, winter's dear!

The Silence That Frosts Us

In silence thick as cozy fleece,
You break the ice, say, "How about cheese?"
With laughter rolling in the brisk air,
We weave through frosty, chilly despair.

The stillness hums a goofy tune,
While we survey the snow, like a cartoon.
A snowdrift's stare can't hold us tight,
We'll dance and twirl, turn cold to light.

Ice-skates squeak like clueless shoes,
As we slip and fall, the world we lose.
We'll turn our stumbles into rhymes,
With each little slip, we craft new chimes.

So here's to silence that frosts our hearts,
It's really just laughter mixed with arts.
In this wintry world, so light and free,
Let's make our chill a harmony.

The Coldness of Unshared Laughter

In the chilly air, we stand apart,
Your giggle's like snow, it warms my heart.
But you hold your joy, like a frosty breath,
While I chuckle alone, it feels like death.

I throw my jokes, but they fall like ice,
You roll your eyes, like rolling dice.
Laughter's a dance, but I'm here to twirl,
With your silent smirk, it's a frozen whirl.

Let's melt the silence, let humor ring,
Forget the snowflakes, and let joy cling.
A punchline shared could warm the air,
Come on, don't leave me with this cold stare.

So shake off the chill, and bust a grin,
In this winter wonder, let the fun begin.
The cold may linger, but let's not be shy,
And laugh until the sun starts to fly.

Winter Winds and Silent Tears

Winter whispers soft, with a frosty sigh,
I'm out here chuckling while you only cry.
Your tears freeze over like ice in a vase,
While I trip on snow, and wear comedy's face.

The wind howls loud, shakes the branches bare,
But I'm busy spinning tales, you're lost in despair.
You wipe your cheeks as I slosh through a joke,
Stumbling and laughing, you just watch and choke.

The snowflakes dance, but your smile's on pause,
I slip on the ice, and you give me the glares.
Can't you just chuckle? It's not so severe,
Yet here I am, cracking up all on my leer.

So let's donhauts to frown, just embrace the freeze,
And sprinkle some giggles with laughter's sweet breeze.
Winter's a time to shine and ignite,
Let's huddle together, and giggle all night.

Shivering Stars Above Us

Stars twinkle bright in this frosty abyss,
I'm making my wishes, but they're met with a hiss.
You lay on the ground, eyes glued to the sky,
I'm chuckling at myself as the cold winds fly.

The cosmos is chilly, but my humor is warm,
Yet you stare at the stars, as if they're the norm.
Throw me a smile, let's blend joy with night,
Instead of just gazing in this starry plight.

My punchlines flicker like distant street lights,
You sigh at the space, while I reach for new heights.
Let's make wishes together, not just sit and wait,
With laughter as bright as the stars up to date.

So hoist up your hopes, let them shine like the sun,
For under these shivers, we'll have way more fun.
In the midnight chill, let's break out in cheer,
And banish the silence, bring giggles near.

Frigid Touches, Warm Longings

Brisk winds caress us, cold fingers entwine,
You shudder away while I jest and rewind.
A frosty encounter, each joke is a fling,
But you glance away, like a winter king.

Your touch sends shivers down my playful spine,
I chuckle and tease, but you stay so benign.
Let's warm up our banter, let's melt down the chill,
In this frozen moment, let's humor fulfill.

I toss you a wink, but the frost lingers near,
While I dance around, you just pout and steer.
The warmth of a chuckle could light up the night,
But your blank expressions leave me in fright.

Come close, share your warmth, let's trade glances anew,
For in shared laughter, we'll chase off the blue.
So grab onto joy, let's melt all we see,
Together in laughter, just you and me.

Warm Longings

In a chilly embrace, our laughter is thin,
You smile like a snowman, hoping to win.
But when the jokes fall, like snowflakes, they break,
I wish for your grin, it's my frozen mistake.

Your silence is icy as winter's cruel breeze,
I'm spinning my humor, but you just freeze.
Come warm up my heart with a giggle or two,
Let's thaw this cold night with laughter that's true.

We tread on the ice, with clumsy delight,
Tripping through winter, can't find what feels right.
Your sigh is a wind, my punchline's a chill,
Together we fumble, let's find the thrill.

So bring on the warmth in this frosty affair,
Let's bundle up laughter, and conquer our glare.
For in every chuckle, a spark can ignite,
Dancing through winter, let's shine in the night.

Frigid Memories Linger

I remember the chill of your icy gaze,
Like a snowman melted in a sunny blaze.
We laughed about mittens, so soft and white,
But how you steal blankets, well, that's just not right.

Your jokes about snowflakes always got me,
I was stuck in the drift while you sipped hot tea.
We'd play in the winter with hats on our heads,
Till I tripped on a snowdrift and fell on my meds.

But remember that time when we built that tall fort?
It collapsed in a second, oh, what a retort!
You blamed it on me, while your cheeks were so red,
That I still can't tell if you laughed or just fled.

So here's to those days when the cold air was bright,
We'll giggle at mishaps while we freeze through the night.

With memories frozen like ice cubes in drink,
Our friendship's a puzzle that sparkles and syncs.

Veil of Crystal Shadows

Under a blanket of shimmering white,
We tiptoe on ice, just don't lose your sight.
Those shadows are dancing, oh what a sight,
But watch your step, buddy, it's slippery tonight!

Remember the snowball that hit me so square?
You laughed like a penguin, oh, what a debonair!
I plotted my sweetest, most careful revenge,
But aiming at you? Well, that was my cringe.

We shared frozen pizzas and watched the world freeze,
While crafting our own little thaw-worthy tease.
The elves in the garden laughed with delight,
As we threw all our worries into the frosty night.

So let's toast to this winter, with cocoa and joy,
To the memories made, we won't ever destroy!
With every misstep and blow to the face,
Each laugh that we shared's a snowflake to trace.

Breath of Winter's Despair

Each breath we exhaled turned to fog in the air,
You grabbed my red scarf, do you even care?
Snowmen were built with a wobbly grin,
They waved goodbye while we slid on the skin.

Remember that skate on the pond, what a sight,
We twirled like lost souls in soft moonlight.
You fell on your backside, and I could not breathe,
I laughed so hard, I was stuck in the weave!

With mittens misplaced and hot drinks gone cold,
We pretended the winter was never too old.
But let's face the truth, in between all the cheer,
We were freezing our tails off and sweating in fear.

So here's to the fumbles, and giggles we made,
Each fall that we took was a bright serenade.
We'll shuffle through snowdrifts and toast to the air,
As winter's breath teaches us not to despair.

Frosted Promises Unkept

You said we'd go sledding, but where did you go?
I waited for hours, it started to snow!
I built you a snowman, it's wearing my hat,
But somehow I think it would rather a chat.

We promised hot cocoa and movies on freeze,
But your pet cat stole the blanket with ease.
We danced with the flakes, each twirl like a dream,
Until we got tangled in quite a cold seam.

The tales we will tell when the thaw starts to call,
Of trips to the ice and the great winter brawl.
With promises frosted like sugar on pies,
We'll laugh till we're old, watch the snow angels rise.

So let's raise our mugs and embrace the cold fun,
With each frozen heartbeat, together we run.
In a world made of winter, my friend, do not fret,
We'll cherish our stories, I'm not done just yet!

Milton Keynes UK
Ingram Content Group UK Ltd.
UKHW021949151124
451186UK00007B/168